SWORD STUDY
ACTIVITY BOOK

Written by
Tammy McMahan

Day 10 Diagram Illustrations by
Doug McGuire

SWORD STUDY
ACTIVITY BOOK

My Name Is:

_____

_____

I Started On:

_____

I Finished On:

_____

Sword Study Activity Book

2012 SWORD STUDY ACTIVITY BOOK
Copyright © 2012 The Shelby Kennedy Foundation
Published by Glass Road Media
First printing February 2013

ISBN: 978-0-9884789-0-9

Dewey Decimal Classification Number: 227

Printed in the United States of America.

For more information about resources for studying the Bible together as a family, or to order additional copies of this resource, visit www.biblebee.org.

Glass Road Media and Management
www.glassroadmm.com

DEDICATION

To the glory and honor of Jesus
Christ, Son of the living God.

For Caroline,
My dear, diligent Timothy.
"Love you more!"

WELCOME

God has important and very helpful truths for you in His Word. As you spend time in His Word alone and together with your family, our prayer is that God will deepen your knowledge of Him and His Word, build and strengthen your relationship with Him, and equip you for the work that He has set forth for you to do! Prepare and get ready for action!

This is what the LORD says:
"Let not the wise man boast of his wisdom or the strong man boast of his strength or the rich man boast of his riches, but let him who boasts boast about this: that he understands and knows me, that I am the LORD, who exercises kindness, justice and righteousness on earth, for in these I delight," declares the LORD.

Jeremiah 9:23-24 (New International Version 1984)

Dear Dad and Mom,

We're so glad that you are investing in Bible study for your whole family! This Activity Book allows the younger members of your family to feel included as they learn essential truths about God at their own level. The book is synchronized with the daily studies of the other three Sword Study levels and is crafted to give your children as much or as little Bible study as they are ready for right now.

Some seven or eight year-old children will feel more comfortable completing this Activity Book independently rather than handling the Primary Sword Study. Most children under seven years will benefit from having you snuggle up beside them and guiding them through the three basic parts of the daily lessons.

Each day starts with a simple prayer in the "Pray" section to teach your child the habit of talking with God. Next, "Color and Do" gives a hands-on activity that reflects the main lesson of the day. "Read and Learn" correlates with the passage that older siblings wrote out that day and begins to plant God's Truth in your young one's mind. The heart symbol finishes with a simple, practical statement to memorize in order to encourage your child to be a "do-er" of God's Word.

Our prayer is that these short lessons prompt longer conversations about Jesus, the Bible and its eternal truths for young disciples. May your entire family be greatly blessed as you gather together around the Living Word of God.

DAY ONE

PRAY... "*Jesus, help* _____
learn about 2 Timothy with our family."

COLOR & DO...

READ & LEARN... 2 Timothy 3:16-17

• The Bible is God's words to us.

• God had men write the words.

• God told the men what to write.

  The Bible is from God to me!

D A Y T W O

PRAY... *"Jesus, help _____ listen closely today."*

COLOR & DO... Write a letter by following each line with a different color.

To: _____

From: _____

READ & LEARN... Acts 9:1-20
• First, Saul was very unkind to Christians.
• Then, he met Jesus on the way to Damascus.
• Now, we call him Paul, a follower of Jesus Christ.

 Paul wrote 2 Timothy.

DAY THREE

PRAY... *"Thank You, Jesus, for loving us."*

COLOR & DO... Draw a stick-figure of Paul below.

Give him... ☐ Hair ☐ Eyes ☐ Nose
☐ Mouth ☐ Shoes

READ & LEARN... John 3:16 and 2 Timothy 2:11
• Paul was a pastor and a teacher.
• Paul told people about Jesus.
• Paul loved Jesus.

Jesus loves me.

DAY FOUR

PRAY... "Jesus, thank you for _____ . Teach him/her about Your words."

COLOR & DO... Mommy and Daddy are your teachers. Color the classroom .

READ & LEARN... 2 Timothy 1:11 and Psalm 119:73-74

• Remember, Paul was a teacher. Timothy was his student.
• 2 Timothy is a letter to Timothy .
• You are a student of the Bible.

   My parents are my teachers.

D A Y   F I V E

PRAY... "Jesus, help _____ be a good listener today."

COLOR & DO... Find the big star where Paul wrote 2 Timothy. Color the map.

Great Sea

*Find the little star where Paul send his letter to Timothy.

READ & LEARN... 2 Timothy 1:8a and Deuteronomy 31:6
• Paul was in a Roman prison.
• Paul was not afraid.
• God was with him.

Do not be afraid. God is always with me.

DAY ONE

PRAY... *"Dear Jesus, thank You for 2 Timothy. Help us follow directions."*

COLOR & DO... Find a "WWJD" item for your young explorer!

MY COPY

JESUS

Practice following the leader

READ & LEARN... 2 Timothy 1:1-2 and 1 Corinthians 11:1

• Paul was an apostle of Jesus.

•An apostle is a follower.

• Followers copy what their leaders do.

Follow what the Bible says!

D A Y T W O

PRAY... *"Jesus, we want to be good students of the Bible. Help us learn Your ways."*

COLOR & DO... We can pray anytime and anywhere!

READ & LEARN... 2 Timothy 1:3-4 and 1 Thessalonians 5:16-18
- Paul prayed for Timothy day and night.
- Praying is talking to God.
- We need to pray to God about our family.

 I can pray to God any time.

DAY THREE

PRAY... *"Dear Jesus, I love being _____'s teacher. Help me to teach him/her well today."*

COLOR & DO... Call your grandma and tell her what you are learning.

Find or draw a picture of your mom and grandma.

READ & LEARN... 2 Timothy 1:5 and Ephesians 6:1-3
* Lois was Timothy's godly grandma.
* Eunice was Timothy's godly mom.
* Grandparents and parents help us to know God.

 God gives us godly teachers.

D A Y   F O U R

PRAY... *"Jesus, help us understand Your Good News."*

COLOR & DO... How do people get news today? Look at a newspaper, email, or the internet. (Parents, have someone send an e-mail to your child.)

READ & LEARN... Romans 3:23, 5:8, 6:23, and 10:13
• God's Good News tell us that our sins can be forgiven!
• We must believe that Jesus died for our sins.
• We must believe in order to be saved from the punishment for our sins.

 ... Whoever calls on Jesus' Name will be saved.

PRAY... *"Jesus, help _____ to understand what the Bible says about You."*

COLOR & DO...*Go lie on the grass and look at the clouds.*

READ & LEARN... Romans 10:9-10

• *Jesus is God's Son.*

• *Jesus came from heaven to earth.*

• *Jesus is our way to heaven.*

 Jesus came to save me.

DAY ONE

PRAY... *"God, You are stronger and more powerful than all men. Thank You for taking care of us."*

COLOR & DO... *Go fly a kite!*

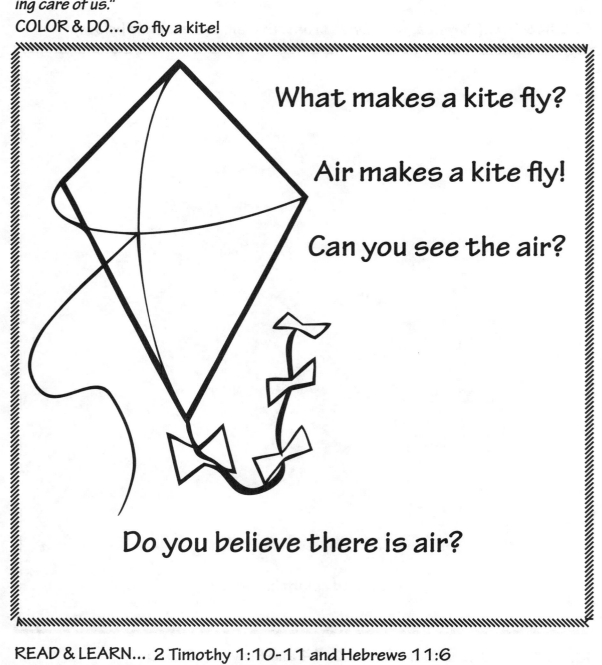

What makes a kite fly?

Air makes a kite fly!

Can you see the air?

Do you believe there is air?

READ & LEARN... 2 Timothy 1:10-11 and Hebrews 11:6

• Faith is believing that Jesus saves us.

• We can't always see things.

• We need to believe even when we can't see.

 My faith in Jesus pleases God.

D A Y   T W O

PRAY...   *"God, help us to trust in You to take care of us."*

COLOR & DO...(Parents, Talk about trust. Explain the example below.)

Trace and color the picture

READ & LEARN... 2 Timothy 1:12-14 and Proverbs 3:5-6
• We don't know everything.
• We need to trust in God.
• God will help us.

    I can trust in God.

D A Y   T H R E E

PRAY... *"Dear Jesus, thank You for our friends and family."*

COLOR & DO... List family and friends out loud. Then draw your best friend.

MY BEST FRIEND

READ & LEARN... 2 Timothy 1:15 and Proverbs 18:24

• *Good friends help each other.*
• *Good friends are kind to each other.*
• *Jesus is the best example of a good friend.*

Jesus will always be my friend.

PRAY... *"Jesus, help _____ be a good friend who shows others how to please You."*

COLOR & DO... Listen for what we learn about God when we study the Bible.

△ 1 John 4:16

God is ❤ _____.

△ Psalm 23:1

God is my 🐑 _____.

△ Psalm 109:21

God is _____.

Fill in the blanks!

READ & LEARN... 2 Timothy 1:16-18

• God is loving.
• God is our Shepherd.
• God is kind and good.

God is good to me.

D A Y   F I V E

PRAY... *"Jesus, thank You for the Bible. Please help _____ pay attention today."*

COLOR & DO... (Encourage your young explorer, and go to a local park. Hold your child's hand and investigate something along the path.)

Good Job, Young Explorer!

READ & LEARN... John 17:17

• God's Word tells us what to do.

• God's Word is like a light.

• God's Word teaches us.

 he Bible is true!

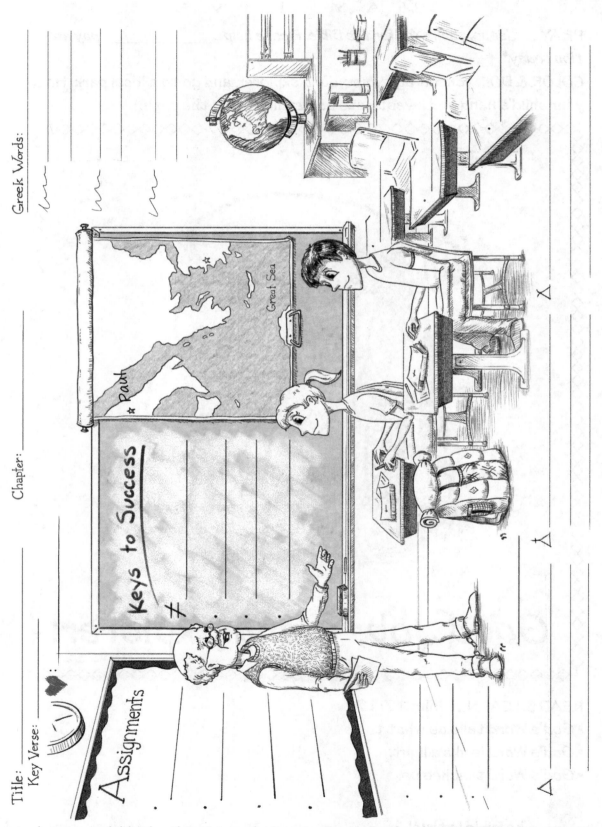

* Parents, have your child color this picture during your Family Bonfire review of 2 Timothy, Chapter 1.

D A Y   O N E

PRAY... *"Lord, You are the Perfect One. All that You tell us is good. Help
_____ obey Your commands."*

COLOR & DO... **What is a command? It is a direction that God gives you.**

Follow the path from the man who talks to the man who listens!

READ & LEARN... 2 Timothy 2:1-4 and Matthew 6:34
• Are you worried about something today?
• We don't need to worry about things today.
• Pray and ask Jesus to help you not feel worried.

Jesus cares if I am worried.

D A Y   T W O

PRAY... *"Jesus, help _____ to follow the rules in the games that he/she plays and that we give him/her."*

COLOR & DO... Play a game of "Mother, May I?"

Play these games with someone older.

Remember to ask about the rules.

READ & LEARN... 2 Timothy 2:5-7

• Rules are important.
• Rules keep us safe.
• We need to obey rules.

Rules should be obeyed with a smile.

DAY THREE

PRAY... *"Jesus, help us to remember all we are learning in 2 TImothy."*

COLOR & DO... (Put five items below on a cookie sheet and cover them.)

We are going to play a game! Ready?!? Look at the cookie sheet for 30 seconds.
Ok... time is up! Circle what you saw.

Did you remember everything you saw?

READ & LEARN... 2 Timothy 2:8-10
- Remember, Jesus died on the cross for our sins.
- Remember, Jesus rose from the dead.
- Remember, Jesus saved us. This is GOOD NEWS!

Remember the Good News of Jesus!

DAY FOUR

PRAY... *"Dear Jesus, thank you for our house. Help _____ understand why Paul tells Timothy to be a prisoner of the Lord."*

COLOR & DO...What is a prisoner? Share why being God's prisoner is positive.

PRISONERS OF THE LORD

READ & LEARN... 2 Timothy 2:11-13 and Ephesians 4:1

• Paul was in prison for talking about God.

• Paul kept working for God even in bad times.

• Being a prisoner for God is good.

 I can be a prisoner of the Lord!

DAY FIVE

PRAY... *"Jesus, You are the Captain of the Christian Army. Help us to be good soldiers for you."*

COLOR & DO... (Parents, talk about soldiers' willingness to protect good.)

Sing & Do Motions
♫ ♫ ♫

I may never march in the ♫ infantry,
ride in the cavalry, ♫
♫ shoot the artillary,
I may never fly over the ♫
♫ enemy,
but I'm in the LORD's
♫ Army!

♫ ♫ ♫ ♫

READ & LEARN... 2 Timothy 2:8-10
• Soldiers of Jesus obey the Bible.
• Soldiers of Jesus love Jesus.
• Soldiers of Jesus tell others about Jesus.

I am a soldier of Jesus.

PRAY... *"Jesus, teach _____ about what it means to be an athlete for You."*

COLOR & DO... (Talk about soldiers. How do they train?)

Do 5 push-ups

Do 5 sit-ups

Race your mom or dad around the house

READ & LEARN... 2 Timothy 2:5-7 and 1 Corinthians 9:24-27

• Athletes practice hard.
• Athletes are healthy.
• Athletes follow the rules.

I am an athlete for God!

DAY TWO

PRAY... *"Dear Jesus, help _____ understand what it means to be like a farmer for you."*

COLOR & DO...Some farmers grow plants; some raise animals. All trust God.

READ & LEARN... 2 Timothy 2:6-7 and Proverbs 24:29-34

• Farmers work hard.

• Farmers are patient.

• Farmers trust God.

I can be like a farmer for Jesus.

DAY THREE

PRAY... *"Dear Jesus, thank You for helping us understand the Bible."*

COLOR & DO...Suffering is having hard days. Sometimes things make us sad.

READ & LEARN... 2 Timothy 2:9 and 2:19

• Paul's days were hard.

• Our days can be hard and sad.

• God is helping us to learn to trust Him on hard days.

Jesus helps me when I suffer.

DAY FOUR

PRAY... *"Lord, You are very patient. Thank You for being patient with us when we don't follow Your words."*

COLOR & DO...Talk about patience. Grab a timer and play!

How long can you...

☐ Hold your breath? _____ seconds

☐ Sing one note? _____ seconds

☐ Open your eyes without blinking? _____ seconds

☐ Keep from complaining? _____ hours

☐ Play the quiet game _____ minutes

READ & LEARN... 2 Timothy 2:24-26

• Patience is waiting for something.
• Patience is waiting for someone.
• Patience does not complain.

It is good for me to be patient.

DAY FIVE

PRAY... *"Today, we want to be careful with our words. Jesus, help us because it can be hard to do."*

COLOR & DO... Shadows: Match each picture to its shadows.

READ & LEARN... 2 Timothy 2:14-15 and Proverbs 15:1

• Kind words make others glad.

• Unkind words make others mad or sad.

• Be slow to talk; think first, then speak.

I need to be careful with my words.

Title: _____
Key Verse: _____
Chapter: _____
Greek Words: _____

SUFFER HARDSHIP LIKE...

RULES

IF _____
THEN _____

* Parents, have your child color this picture during your Family Bonfire review of 2 Timothy, Chapter 2.

DAY ONE

PRAY... *"Jesus, help us to be people who love You more than anything else."*

COLOR & DO... Opposites

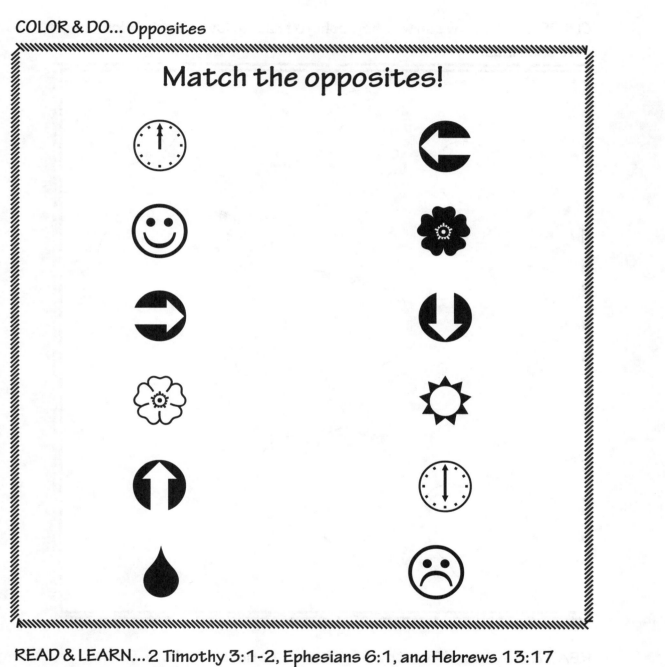

READ & LEARN... 2 Timothy 3:1-2, Ephesians 6:1, and Hebrews 13:17

• We can disobey God's words.

• We can obey God's words.

• We show God that we love Him when we obey.

 I want to obey God.

D A Y   T W O

PRAY... *"Jesus, help us love You more every day."*

COLOR & DO... How can we show others that we love them? Color a heart with each idea.

READ & LEARN... 2 Timothy 3:3-5 and 1 Corinthians 13:3-5
• We show others love by being kind to them.
• We show others love by doing things for them.
• We show God love by obeying HIm.

want to love God more each day!

DAY THREE

PRAY... "It is a new day. Thank you Jesus for giving _____ and me this time together to learn about You."

COLOR & DO... What does it mean to listen?

What sounds do these animals make? Make the sound and then color the creature!

READ & LEARN... 2 Timothy 3:7, Proverbs 7:24, and Proverbs 12:15

• Listening is important.

• A person who is listening is not talking.

• Looking into someone's eyes shows that we are listening.

When I listen, I can understand directions.

DAY FOUR

PRAY... *"God, You are amazing. You know everything. Teach us more from 2 Timothy today."*

COLOR & DO... What are you thankful for? Do we thank Jesus enough?

READ & LEARN... 2 Timothy 3:8-9 and Psalm 9:1-4

• *Give thanks to Jesus for all He gives you.*

• *Tell others all about Jesus' good works.*

• *Sing praises to Him.*

I need to tell Jesus "Thank You" everyday!

DAY FIVE

PRAY... *"Jesus, You are good to forgive us when we disobey and say we are sorry. Thank You for Your love."*

COLOR & DO... Good students listen to their teachers.

Write something the Bible tells you to do on the chalkboard above.

READ & LEARN... 2 Timothy 3:10-11, Luke 6:40, John 13:13
• You are a student of Daddy and Mommy.
• You are a student of the Bible.
• You are a student of Jesus.

I need to be a good student!

D A Y   O N E

PRAY... *"Thank You for talking to us in the Bible. It is wonderful to know You are so great and care about me."*

COLOR & DO... Turn to Psalm 119:1-7 to look at different names of God's Word.

Names for God's Word

- _____

- _____

- _____

- _____

- _____

- _____

READ & LEARN... 2 Timothy 3:14-15 and Psalm 119:10-11

• God's Word helps us do the right thing.

• God's Word tells us that Jesus loves us.

• God's Word give us wisdom.

...God's Word is very helpful.

D A Y   T W O

PRAY... *"Jesus, You always tell the truth. Help us to be like You. Help us to tell the truth."*

COLOR & DO... *What is the Bible? Do you remember? Read and color the daisy.*

THE BIBLE IS...

...but the *Word* of our GOD stands FOREVER. ~Isaiah 40:8~ KJV

GOD'S WORD

READ & LEARN...2 Timothy 3:16-17 and John 17:17

• God gave us His words in the Bible.

• God's words are true.

• God's words tell me what to do.

 I want to follow God's words.

DAY THREE

PRAY... "Jesus, You are so faithful. Thank You for always being with us. Teach us to be excited to learn about You."

COLOR & DO... The Bible helps us to be good. Connect the dots from 1 to 37.

READ & LEARN... Psalm 119:9 and Isaiah 40:8

• God's Word helps us to do good things.

• God's Word lasts forever.

• God's Word is powerful.

 I need to learn God's Word.

DAY FOUR

PRAY... *"God, You created everything we see. You created us. We are so thankful for everything You made."*

COLOR & DO... Sometimes we disobey. We need to tell God that we are sorry.

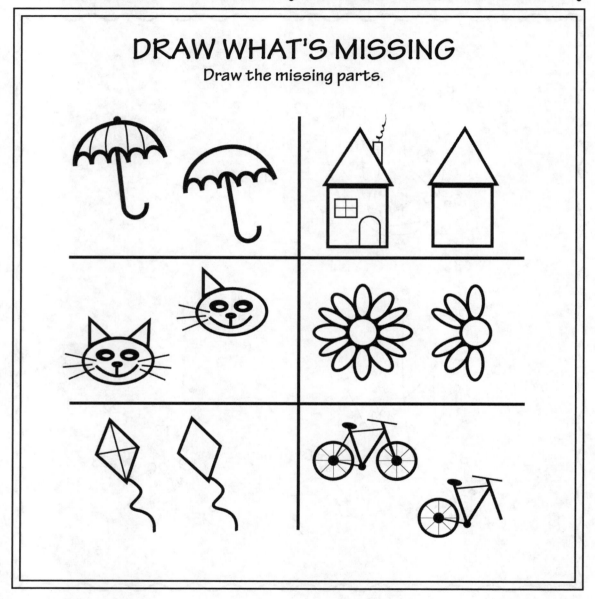

DRAW WHAT'S MISSING
Draw the missing parts.

READ & LEARN... 2 Timothy 3:16-17 and 1 John 1:9

• The Bible tells us what is wrong.

• Sometimes we do the wrong thing and sin.

• We can tell God anything.

God loves me no matter what.

DAY FIVE

PRAY... *"Jesus, help_____ be kind when others are unkind to him/her."*

COLOR & DO... "Persecute" is a big word that means being unkind to others.

BE KIND TO OTHERS!

READ & LEARN... 2 Timothy 3:10-12 and Luke 6:35

• Sometimes people are unkind to us.

•Jesus helps when others are unkind to us.

• We need to be kind to others.

Jesus is kind and wants me to be kind, too!

Title: _____
Key Verse: _____

PROFITABLE FOR

Chapter: _____
:

NAMES

Greek Words:
~~~~~ _____
~~~~~ _____

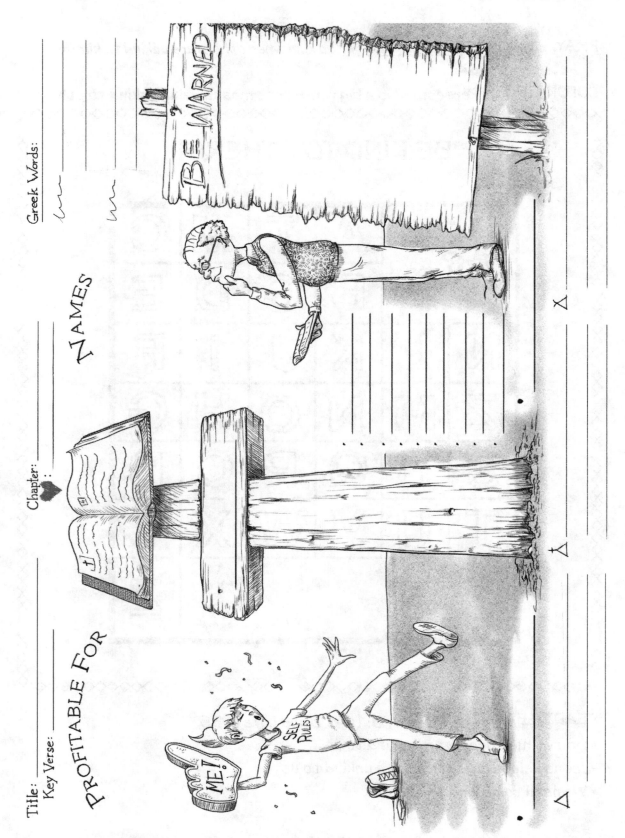

BE WARNED

SELF RULES

ME!

△ _____

△ _____

△ _____

* Parents, have your child color this picture during your Family Bonfire review of 2 Timothy, Chapter 3.

50

DAY ONE

PRAY... *"Jesus, thank You for_____. I am so thankful for him/her. Help us learn more today."*

COLOR & DO... Be ready! When? All the time. For what? To share God's Word!

Be ready to tell others about the GOOD NEWS in all seasons!

Fill in the boxes with your own pictures for the other seasons.

READ & LEARN... 2 Timothy 4:1-2

• We can <u>share</u> the Good News about Jesus.

• We need to be ready to <u>share</u> anytime.

• We need to be ready to <u>share</u> all the time.

I am ready to tell others about Jesus.

D A Y   T W O

PRAY... *"Dear Jesus, we are a little tired today. Give us energy to listen and learn about You."*

COLOR & DO... The Bible is true. The Bible is not made up.

True or False?

The story of the three pigs... True or False

The story of Noah and the ark... True or False

The story of Goldilocks and the three bears... True or False

The story of Bo Peep... True or False

The story of Jonah... True or False

The story of Jesus... True or False

All of the Bible stories are TRUE!

READ & LEARN... 2 Timothy 4:3-5 and Titus 1:2-3
• People do not always tell the truth.
• God always tells the truth.
• The Bible is true.

 I can believe the Bible!

D A Y   T H R E E

PRAY... *"We have so much, Lord! We have our house, beds, and yummy food for meals. Thank You for taking care of us."*

COLOR & DO... Kings wear crowns. Winners wear crowns. Decorate this crown.

Decorate the crown with crayons and stickers. You could even glue craft materials on it.

READ & LEARN... 2 Timothy 4:7-8, Proverbs 17:6

• Crowns are a reward for doing something well.

• God gives crowns in heaven for doing well.

• You are the crown to your grandparents.

Crowns are rewards for doing right actions.

53

DAY FOUR

PRAY... *"Dear Jesus, we are hearing so many things in Your Bible. Help us to be good doers and workers, too."*

COLOR & DO... Friends are gifts from God.

READ & LEARN... 2 Timothy 4:9-10, Proverbs 17:17a, and 1 Thessalonians 3:2

• Friends cheer us up when we are sad.

• Friends help us.

• Good friends love Jesus, too.

I can be a good friend.

DAY FIVE

PRAY... *"Dear Jesus, thank You for giving _____ so many people in his/ her life that cheer for him/her."*

COLOR & DO... *God gives us people who encourage us like a cheering crowd.*

Draw your greatest encouragers on the podiums. Put the names of others in the stands.

READ & LEARN... 2 Timothy 4:11-16

• *God made people.*

• *God loves people.*

• *We need to love people by encouraging them.*

I can tell my friends, "Have a good day! Jesus loves you!"

DAY ONE

PRAY... *"Lord, You are everlasting, strong and never get tired. Thank You for always watching over us."*

COLOR & DO... Preachers tell others about God.

Paul was a preacher.
Timothy was a preacher.

You can be a preacher, too!

READ & LEARN... 2 Timothy 4:1-2 and Acts 1:8

• People who tell others about God are preaching.

• People who tell others about God are preachers.

• God loves it when we preach.

I am thankful for preachers in my life.

D A Y   T W O

PRAY... *"The Bible tells us that goodness comes to those who walk in Your ways. Help us to do what You say."*

COLOR & DO...Who is your pastor? He is a preacher and teacher of the Word!

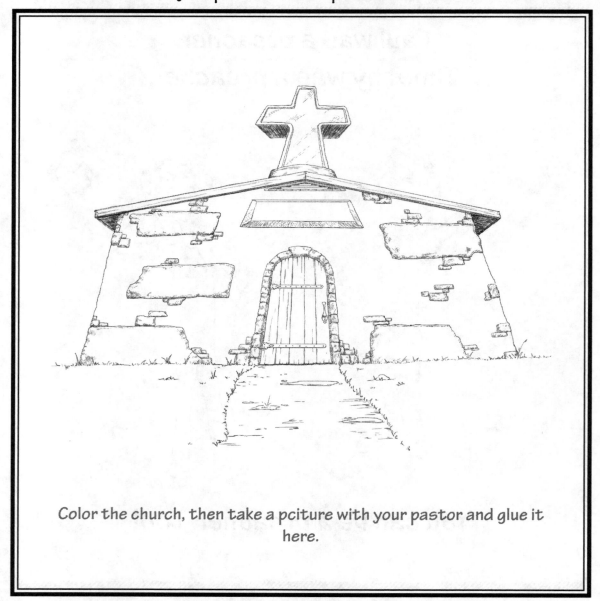

Color the church, then take a pciture with your pastor and glue it here.

READ & LEARN...1 Timothy 5:17 and 2 Timothy 4:16-17
- *God gave us a preacher in our church.*
- *Our preacher teaches us God's Word.*
- *Good preaching makes our hearts strong.*

    I am thankful for my preacher.

DAY THREE

PRAY... *"Jesus, You are the most important person who ever lived on the earth. Thank You for being our friend."*

COLOR & DO...Remember patience? Patience is waiting without complaining.

Jesus will come back in the clouds. Draw the sun, clouds and Jesus coming back.

We have to be ready, but with patience.

READ & LEARN... 2 Timothy 4:18 and John 14:2-3
- Jesus is coming back to earth.
- Jesus is going to bring His children to heaven.
- Heaven is a beautiful place!

Jesus is coming back!

DAY FOUR

PRAY... *"Lord, help us think of friends who need our help today. We want to do something kind to help show Your love to others."*

COLOR & DO... Serving others shows God's love.

Call a friend

Bake some cookies

Send a letter

God uses people to show His love

READ & LEARN...2 Timothy 4:20-22 and Galatians 5:13

• Visiting someone who is sick shows God's love.

• Bringing a meal to a family who has a new baby shows God's love.

• Sending a letter to a lonely friend shows God's love.

I can show others Jesus' love today.

DAY FIVE

PRAY... *"Today is going to be a busy day. Help _____ and me slow down and enjoy being with You in the Bible."*

COLOR & DO... Your life is like a race. Run well by learning God's Word!

Go to a park or your backyard.

☐ **Run around a tree**

☐ **Jump over something**

☐ **Swing on a swing**

☐ **Skip down a path**

READ & LEARN... 2 Timothy 4:7

• Our life is like a race.

• We start when we are born.

• God wants to be our Coach.

I need to run a good race.

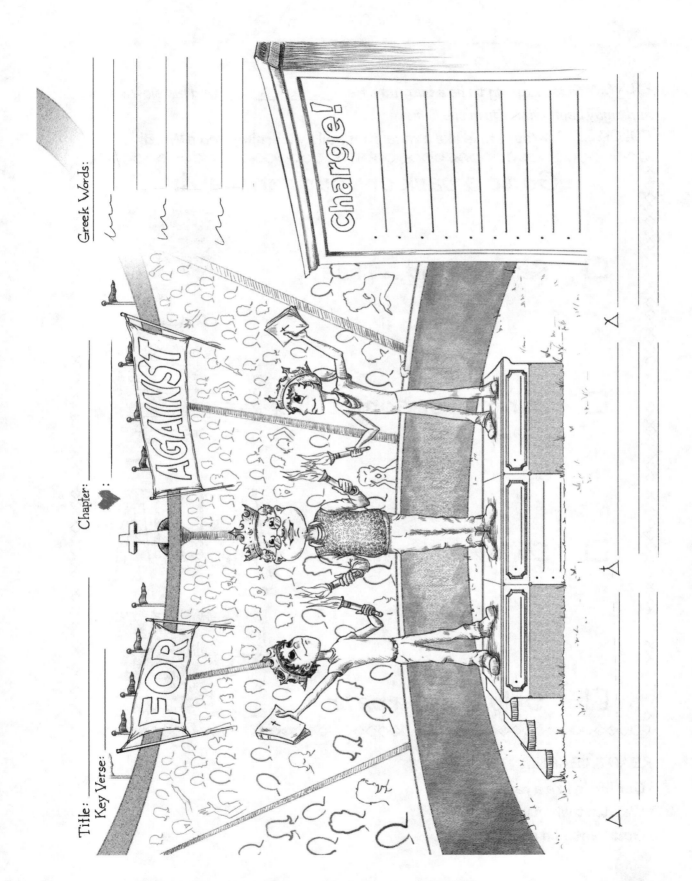

* Parents, have your child color this picture during your Family Bonfire review of 2 Timothy, Chapter 4.

DAY ONE

PRAY... *"Jesus, thank You for another day learning about 2 Timothy with _____ . We are glad to be learning Your words."*

COLOR & DO... Stand up for what is right. The Bible gives us directions.

READ & LEARN... 2 Timothy 1:8 and Deuteronomy 31:6

• Stand up for what is right.
• Tell others about Jesus.
• God is the One who is with you always.

My God is strong!

DAY TWO

PRAY... *"God, You are the King of all the Kings. Help us serve and worship You through how we live."*

COLOR & DO... Be a good workman for God. Learn about God!

READ & LEARN... 2 Timothy 2:15

• Good workers work hard.

• Good workers are cheerful and obedient.

• Good workers finish what they start.

   I want to be a good worker!

DAY THREE

PRAY... *"Jesus, thank You for talking to me through the Bible. Help us to love Your words more."*

COLOR & DO... The Bible is the most important book.

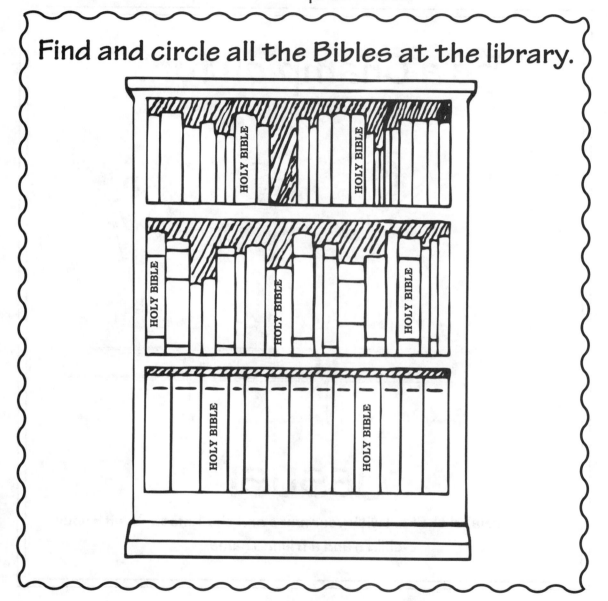

Find and circle all the Bibles at the library.

READ & LEARN... 2 Timothy 3:16-17 and Ecclesiastes 12:12-13

• Men have written lots of books.

• God wrote one book.

• God's book is the best book.

The Bible is the most important book!

DAY FOUR

PRAY... *"jesus, when we are sad, glad, mad or happy, You want to hear from us in prayer. Thank You for listening."*

COLOR & DO...

Be a Champion for...

JESUS!

Parents, label the Paul with your name and the Timothy's with your child's and a friends name.

READ & LEARN... 2 Timothy 4:7-8

• God wants us to serve Him.

• God wants us to trust Him.

• God wants us to love Him.

I can be one of God's Champions!

DAY FIVE

PRAY... *"Jesus, keep bringing _____ near to You. Help us keep digging in Your Bible."*

COLOR & DO... Great job, young explorer!

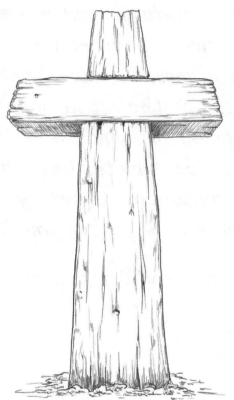

Remember the
Good News!

READ & LEARN... John 3:16 and Romans 5:8

• Jesus loves you.

• Jesus wants you to believe in Him.

• Jesus is the Good News.

 Jesus loves me most!

CONGRATULATIONS!

You are at the finish line of
this race! Well done!

*Many times in life the end of one thing is
the beginning of another. We hope that
will be true here. You have finished this
study of 2 Timothy but we hope that you
will never finish studying the Bible. The end
of this study can be the beginning of the
adventure of studying your
Bible for the rest of your life!*

What book will you pick next?

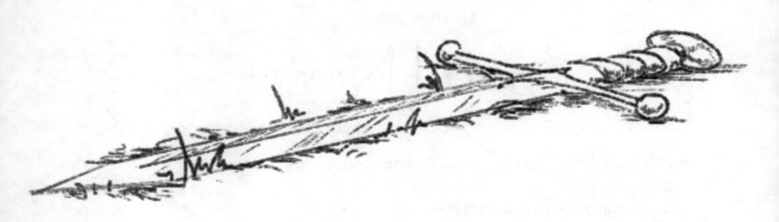